Poems From Me to You

By

Keke LiBron

ISBN : 978-1-962224-12-3

printed in the United States of America

"POEMS FROM ME TO YOU" IS A POETIC

REFLECTION OF OUR TIME AS SEEN THROUGH

MY EYES AND FELT IN MY HEART AND SPIRIT.

ENJOY.

Keke LiBron

Synopsis

Poetry is the song without the external instrumentals. Its beat is voice, the heart, the eyes, hands, feet and fingers.

Poetry is the emotions we try to find words for, though words are limiting.

Like the adolescent cutter who inflicts pain on themselves to release their inner turmoil. In poetry the pen is the razor, the arm is our paper and the blood is our words.

In times of joy our sweet tears becomes the ink.

Poems from Me to You is a work I started as a teen and expanded on. In it you can see my growth in life and writing. When others knew I was going to publish my work they asked if their work could be included. So, it has been

One poem was given to me by Bob Norris at his Hospitality House in Texas. The guy who wrote it was on Death Row. After he was put to death by lethal injection they found out he was innocent. I never got to meet him but his words touch me today as they did the first day I read them. His poem is one of my favorites and I have read it in various venues in New York City.

Dedication

This book is dedicated to the Great Spirit, the I AM that lives in me and creates through me.

My Great-Grandmother Ada Marshall LiBron who made sure we knew who we are. I love you so much.

To the fruit of my womb; my daughter, Dimin, thank you for making me a mother, "Ti amo in questa vita e nella prossima."

To my son, Jason, "I love you seven."

Thank you both for choosing me. May I always make you proud.

And, to Gerald Schultz, we started this project together and we are finishing it together. I love you.

Acknowledgments

Thanks to the MOST HIGH

Thanks to my mother, my father, Hilary Gibbs,

Bob and Nelda Norris, Peter Lemmo,

Gerald Schultz, all the poets who contributed

their work to add variety to

this book, and to everyone at Evander Childs

High School, thanks for just listening.

I would also like to publicly thank my professors at Herbert H. Lehman College.

Your teaching, knowledge, and guidance have stayed with me, and I pass it on to others.

Thank you, Professor Billy Collins, who looked me in my eyes and said,

"In your search to be poetic, don't lose the poem." I never forgot this and never will.

I love you for this.

Thank you, Professor Blanco, who taught me,

"Don't let anyone tell you you're saying Salmon wrong." I stick it to everyone who challenges me.

About the Author

I am an indigenous American. My maternal line is Blackfoot. My paternal great grandmother was Cherokee. I was born in The Bronx/Rananchqua after my mother went into labor on the 2 or 5 train. The nearest hospital was Jacobi.

My parents were born on Manahatta, now known as Manhattan, Harlem specifically. My father was Cherokee and Irish.

I have two beautiful children; they're my greatest accomplishments.

I graduated from Dewitt Clinton High School, my Speech, Writing and Drama teacher was Mrs. Sandy Skodnik. I Majored in English at Herbert H. Lehman College,with a Minor in Education and a Specialization in Creative Writing. I completed course work for my Master's Degree in Adolscent Counseling at Cambridge College.

I have been writing all my life. One of my first poems was published in our school news paper while I attended Lorraine Hansberry Middle School. I started to save my writings around the age of thirteen.

Foreword

This book is a collection of work from America's great young artists. The writings are an expression of life in New York City.

I have known Keke for many years and am proud to say that her approach to many topics covered is expressive and unique.

If thought-provoking writing is your favor, then read on. In times of indecision and hostility, it's good to

experience a positive attitude and love of humanity; this is the essence of this book.

Gerald Schultz

New York Fashion Photographer

Talk Show Host

Entrepreneur

Contents

I think this was written in 1997

A Description of Self

Tall, lean, and strong, with brown skin reflecting
the dominance of those who came before her.

Jet black thick spiral curly hair that once hung on
her back.

Brown almond-shaped eyes, with black eyelashes
that touch black eyebrows, passed down from her
Grandma Ada.

A brown nose with nostrils that form the shape of a
w.

Small ears placed carefully on the sides of her
head.

Top lip from her father, bottom lip from her
mother, soft, sexy, and full.

Long, thin, veiny muscular arms run on like a path
to lengthy branch-like slim fingers; a scar on the
middle one reminds her of her playful youth. Pure
white fingernails like those done up in a French
Manicure but they're not.

Caramel-colored breasts, no bigger than a mouth
full.

Nipples, the size of a dime, sit like chocolate-
covered raisins in caramel

Muscles that favor ice cubes all in a row sit side by side in a tray.

The navel that once joined her to the source of her darkness and the mark left

By Chicken Pox when she was twelve.

A path of black hair leads you to her triangle of black bush and candied apple warmth.

Buttocks shaped like a heart in a 'g' string. The biggest part of her.

Thighs like those of a stallion give way to a ball of brown calf.

Wide feet not accustomed to the shoe of the European long for the energy of the earth. Mother Earth knows her children.

I AM a description you cannot escape. I AM your mother, your sister, your girlfriend, a forbidden fruit to some who dream up fantasies of copper goddesses who look just like me.

1997

WHERE I COME FROM

I COME FROM A TIME OF QUEENS AND KINGS

FROM A LAND RICH IN GOLD AND PRECIOUS STONES.

I COME FROM A TIME WHERE FRUIT GREW ABUNDANTLY

AND ALL MY NEEDS WERE MET.

A TIME WHEN ELEPHANTS AND ZEBRA ROAMED OUTSIDE MY HOME.

WHERE GIRAFFES AND BEAUTIFUL BIRDS WOULD COME FOR ME TO PET.

I COME FROM A TIME WHEN WE TRADED WITH OTHER INDIANS

EVERYTHING FROM SKINS AND STONES, FROM SPEARS TO GENETIC MATERIAL.

WHEN CIVILIZATION EXISTED, AND SO DID PEACE AND HARMONY.

I COME FROM A TIME OF AFRICA'S DRUMBEAT AND TRIBAL DANCE.

A TIME WHEN WE WORE TURQUOISE AND RED STONES

AND IN A CIRCLE, THE INDIANS WOULD PRANCE.

WHEN COLORED FEATHERS HUNG FROM
MY ANKLE AND NECK.

I COME FROM A TIME WHEN WE PRAYED
FOR RAIN, AND IT RAINED,

AND RAINED, AND RAINED UNTIL I
PRAYED FOR IT TO STOP

AND IT DID.

August 29, 1996

Dance Africa's Dance

When I See Africa dance

my heart races.

Blood rushes through my Veins

and my Soul Starts to dance

my every Step is in Sync

with her musical Vibe

though I've Never Set

Foot on her Soil

I know the drum

The ancestors will not allow

Me to Forget

they linger over me, around

me, and within me.

Pushing my body to her

beat

they have risen

and every Fiber, every cell, every tissue, every
nerve

Has awakened within me, until I too

am dancing Africa's dance.

1996

Today

New lives dwelling amongst
the old
That's the way it should be
so that knowledge and tradition
is passed on.
Today it's hard to know
who will die First,
the young or the old.....
the old seem to outlive the
young.
A life of Struggle and of
pain.
My insides turn into knots
saliva feels like a dry rock
passing down my throat
the fear of the unknown
is sometimes frightening
it's hard when I don't
who will die next, my
grandmother or my Mother

my uncle or my brother
my sister or my daughter
I don't know when, where
or whom.
Today
The beginning is so close to
the End.
The beginning is the End...
Today could be the End.

Dedicated to Lori and Michael Shinn

Untitled

The world we live in
different nationalities
different cultures
different traditions
different concepts of life
but one people
only one goal
to get ahead
to live comfortably
happily
to be able to witness
the evolution
of its forever-changing years
known to all as
the turn of time, time, time, time.....

BlackPete/Sanchez/Poppie
1980

"I am"

I am a prisoner
I am of a poor people
I am Black
I am Puerto Rican
I am a Man
I am a Friend
I am who I wish to be
I am Another Human Being.

Black Pete/Sanchez/Poppie

February 27, 1982

Summertime in the Bronx

Summertime in the Bronx
can be a lot of fun, especially
if you're a Kid.
Summertime in the Bronx
is watching people on stoops
fan themselves with newspapers
or cardboard.
Summertime in the Bronx
is waiting for the next cool
breeze to sneak up on you
it's jumping in and out of
an open fire hydrant
to cool off on a 90° day
drinking gallons of water, and
buying ice cream cones, and
Sundaes from the Good
Humor truck.
Summertime in the Bronx
is going to the pool with
Sweaty friends, talking about

the cold of winter, and
waiting for the Sun to
go down when everyone
and everything has cooled off.
Summertime in the Bronx
is plain ol' Summertime
in the Bronx....then
comes winter. (Brrrr)

December 16, 1986

To Christmas

To Christmas is to
Love and Show Love
It is a gathering of family
and Loved ones

To Christmas:
of all the holidays
within the year you
are the one who brings
my family near, the
Loudest of Laughter lingers
in the air, with
Christmas Carols being
sung everywhere, telling us
that Christmas is near...
that Christmas is Here!

To Christmas is to do
all these things, and
more in a day
then as though yesterday
Never existed comes
Tomorrow.

May 28, 1983

The Math of Life

Divide your attention;
add your knowledge;
multiply your kind;
subtract all frustrations;
meditate and
always share.

THE INVISIBLE GOLDEN KEY

THE CLOUDS IN THE SKY ARE LIKE THE UNLOCKED SOULS THAT THE PHYSICAL REALM HAS UNLEASHED TO THEIR MYSTICAL ETERNAL HOME.

THE WHITE ELEGANT INSPIRING CLOUDS ARE AS OF THE SOULS WHO'VE FOUND ETERNAL

LIFE AND HAPPINESS, AND NOW THEIR SPIRITS ROAM PEACEFULLY AND FREE LIKE AN EAGLE

IN THE SKY, GLIDING EASILY OVER THE TALL FOREST TREES, PRAISING GOD AND ENJOYING WHAT HE HAS GIVEN THEE.

BEFORE THEY PASSED ON TO A MUCH GREATER EXISTENCE, THEY WERE GIVEN THE MOST CRUCIAL, INVISIBLE GOLDEN KEY. JUST READ JOHN CHAPTER 3:16, AND YOULL KNOW WHAT THIS TRULY MEANS.

THE DARK, DEPRESSING CLOUDS ARE AS OF THE LOST MORBID SOULS WHO'VE FOUND WITH EXCRUCIATING PAIN AND ETERNAL TORMENT, THEY MUST HATE THEIR AFTERLIFE, THEY MUST MOURN IT.

ALL OF THIS BECAUSE THEIR DOORS OF PERCEPTION WEREN'T WILLING ENOUGH TO SEE

WHAT GOD WAS HOLDING RIGHT IN FRONT OF THEIR FACE, THAT MOST CRUCIAL GOLDEN KEY.

OH, IN CASE YOU DON'T KNOW WHAT JOHN 3:16 TRUTHFULLY MEANS, LET ME EXPLAIN IT TO YOU BEFORE YOUR LIFETIME ON EARTH ENDS.

IT MEANS WE MUST HAVE BLIND FAITH THAT JESUS HAS FORGIVEN US FOR OUR SINS.

WHEN THE TIME COMES, YOU WILL SEE THE FINAL RESTING PLACE YOUR SOUL WILL BE.

YOU CANNOT RUN, AND YOU DEFINITELY CAN NOT HIDE, IF YOUVE LIVED THE LIFE YOU

SHOULD'VE AND YOUR TIME COMES, YOU SHALL GLADLY AWAIT THE INEVITABLE ANGEL

OF DEATH TO ESCORT YOU TO THE OTHER SIDE.

THINK ABOUT IT; THIS LIFE ISNT AS BAD AS IT SEEMS. JUST THINK OF IT AS A STERLING

STEPPING STONE THAT BRINGS US CLOSER TO OUR DREAMS. MY GOD HAS ASSURED ME

THAT NOT EVEN ALL OF SATAN'S EVIL AND ALL OF HIS FOLLOWERS HATE CAN NOT STOP

ME FROM PASSING THROUGH THOSE GOLDEN AND PEARLY GATES.

I WONDER, LORD JESUS, WHAT WILL IT BE LIKE THERE? WHAT WILL WE SEE? WHAT MIRACLES

WILL THIS ELITE FORCE AND I WITNESS WITH THIS GOLDEN KEY YOU HAVE GIVEN THEE?

WE MUST PRAY FOR THE SOULS WHO STILL WEAR THEIR PHYSICAL GARMENTS, THAT THEY ARE WISE ENOUGH TO GRASP THAT GOLDEN KEY, THE ONE AND ONLY THAT BRINGS A CELEBRATION FOR US CHRISTIANS

FOR THE REST OF ETERNITY.

CHRISTOPHER JONES

October 24, 1992

Dream Come True

As I Slept, I dreamt
what I dreamt of, I could
not remember.
Then I dreamed again,
of Fish and Rain of a
pretty small white dove
As I dreamed, I smiled
I didn't know why, but I did
I remembered the dream
When you were born, because
it was you I was dreaming of
My Little Love, My Pretty
brown dove.

4:31 A.M. August 18, 1990
S5lbs. 10Oz.
Welcome to the World, baby girl

December 21, 1992
Approximately 9 a.m.

Untitled

Sometimes I've wished
I'd Sleep, never to awake
I'd Leave all my troubles
and worries behind.
As I Float, Smiling Toward
That Big Gate
Happiness would be everlasting.
worries no more
As I glide on heavens
cloudy floor
I have a daughter, though
and Lots to see
things are left in a mess,
and that's not like Me.
I wake to unveil a new
day and realize I wasn't
ready anyway.

March 13, 1993

DAD

Ten years passed, and I'd thought
I had no dad.
At last, I've Found you but
how long will you last?
Your body's weak, and your head is
bald, Ten years dad and
not one call.
I've waited For this moment
As each year passed me by
I'm delighted to be here with you,
but ALL I can do
is cry.

November 2, 1992

Mind Talk

You said if I ever needed
you and you weren't there
that I should use my mind, and you would
hear.
Well, I'm calling you but
it seems to be to no avail.
I won't stop trying though
cause I can hear you
Loud and Clear
LOUD AND CLEAR

August 4, 1996

Orchard Beach

I sat in my room
all day long

I could see the sun
Peeping through the vertical
blinds,
spots of sunlight
On the floor trying to
Shine upon my gloom

it couldn't reach through my
bed was on the other side
of the room, too far

the phone was turned off,
I don't wanna talk to
nobody anyway

Somebody calling with
Some good news

I don't wanna Smile,
I don't need no one
Shining on my gloom

Today would be perfect
if only it would rain,
rain on my gloom
I wish it would rain,
Why won't it RAIN!

SUNSHINE AND RAIN

I ASK MYSELF QUESTIONS, AND THE
ANSWER IS PLAIN,

WOULD I ENJOY THE SUNSHINE IF I DIDN'T
HAVE RAIN?

OR IF LIFE HAD NO HEARTACHES, AND I
LIVED WITHOUT LOSS,

WOULD I SEEK FOR HIS COMFORT AT THE
FOOT OF THE CROSS?

AND IF THERE WAS NO WINTER TO
FREEZE ME WITH FEAR,

WOULD I YEARN FOR THE WARMTH OF
SPRING EVERY YEAR?

AND IF ALL THAT I WANTED WAS THERE
EVERY DAY,

WOULD I KNEEL BEFORE GOD AND
EARNESTLY PRAY?

OR IF I NEVER KNEW SICKNESS AND
NEVER FELT PAIN,

WOULD I REACH FOR HIS HAND TO HELP
AND SUSTAIN?

AND IF I HAD NO TEARDROPS RUNNING
DOWN TO THE FLOOR,

WOULD I CRY TO MY FATHER AND SEEK
HIM YET MORE?

SO IF I HAD NO TRIALS TO COME DOWN
MY WAY,

WOULD I KNEEL BEFORE GOD AND
EARNESTLY PRAY?

SO I ASK MYSELF QUESTIONS, AND THE
ANSWER IS PLAIN,

WOULD I ENJOY THE SUNSHINE IF I NEVER
HAD RAIN?

EILSEO H. MORENO

EXECUTED MARCH 4, 1987

October 24, 1995

Mind's Eye

I have made love to you a
thousand times
So many times
a srong, passionate love
with my eyes meeting with your
eyes
My lips softly kissing your lips
Uhmmmm
My warm moist body pressed
firmly against yours
I have felt your soft skin
and smelled your cologne
I have made love to you a
thousand times.
I have felt the power of your
love deep within, causing a
pain of my right side as
I throw my head back and
receive you.
I have made

love to you a thousand times
over and over
again a thousand times
All in my mind's eye.

January 11, 1991

Sold Soul

You gave the devil Your
Soul
Now he Rules you through your
nose
Each and every day, you say
tomorrow, tomorrow I'll turn away
But tomorrow never comes;
just another today.
You gave the Devil your
Soul
Now he rules you through your
Nose
You run the streets while others
are asleep, your face looks old
your body's weak
you're hurting me yet you
refuse to See.
All you see in your Mind
are 1, 2, 3, or 10 more Lines.
You gave the Devil your

Soul
now He rules you through your
Nose.
You ask for a chance
to get on your feet but
you didn't call on the Most
High, who could help you
in your defeat
So now you're back on
the streets.
You gave the Devil the Soul
I Pray you get it Back.

March 5, 1997

"The You Within You"

I wanna know
the real you
The one that Smiles cause
it wants to, not because everyone
expects it, or even that you should.

The Real You, the you that
can't hide what it feels
the you that flows through
your eyes, your arms, and your
touch.
The within who's scared
but whose surface looks so
unafraid.

The you that has thoughts
and feelings unallied with
the thoughts and feelings of
the face.
The within that's crying
but has no tears

The You Within You
Set it Free, let it go
get to know the Me Within Me.

September 24, 1992

The Mechanic and Me

I laid there like a car
being worked on
tears ran from my eyes
as I wished it had never
happened
the mechanic went to work
under the hood, exposing my
engine
the sounds of the tools
hitting each other still ring in
my head, sounds I never will
forget.
my palms began to moisten
beads of sweat form on
my head as the pain caused
me to tense up, I
balled my fists, but I
was supposed to be a car
on the outside, I was shining
and brand new

but on the inside, I was
wearing down fast.
I wanted to be strong,
but I'm not sure for whom
the mechanic, or myself
perhaps it was for me.
since I had made the decision
to be there, perhaps it was for
him, for his words of approval
"you're doing fine."

TO MY FAMILY AT BRONX KINSHIP

SO LONG TO MY FAMILY
WHOM I LOVE SO MUCH
I PROMISE TO ALWAYS
STAY IN TOUCH.
YOU ALL HAD A HAND
IN HELPING ME GROW
I'M SAD TO BE LEAVING
BUT ITS TIME TO GO.
SO MANY PERSONALITIES
COMING TOGETHER AS ONE
IT HAS REALLY BEEN A PLEASURE
AND SO MUCH FUN.
WE'VE SHARED SOME GOOD TIMES,
SOME SAD ONES TOO
AND THROUGH THEM ALL
WE STUCK TOGETHER LIKE GLUE
I LOVE YOU, I'LL MISS YOU
AND I WANT YOU TO SEE
YOU EACH MEAN SOMETHING
VERY SPECIAL TO ME.
I ASK THAT YOU REMEMBER ME

AS I REMEMBER YOU
MY FAMILY AT BRONX KINSHIP,
SOUTHERN BOULEVARD CREW.
LOVE FROM PAM CLARKE

WHAT KIND OF MAN I AM

DAMN, YOU'VE HEARD MY EXPRESSION.
NOW TELL ME WHAT KIND OF MAN I AM.

I AM THE LEAST FEARED MAN ON EARTH.
EVERY DAY IS OPEN SEASON AS

WE ARE PREYED UPON FROM BIRTH.

NO LONGER CAN YOU SAY THE WORD
CONSPIRACY, IT'S NO LONGER

POLITICALLY CORRECT, WHICH MEANS SO
MANY MORE LIVES WILL BE

WRECKED.

DAMN, YOU'VE HEARD MY EXPRESSION.
NOW TELL ME WHAT KIND OF MAN I AM.

A MAN WHO WILL FOREVER BE
UNDERPAID.

A MAN WHO APPEARS TO BE BRAVE BUT
LIVES HIS LIFE SO AFRAID.

WE WERE TOLD TO FORGET ALL THE
YEARS WE SLAVED AND ALL OUR

GREAT CIVILIZATIONS WHILE OTHERS
LIVED ENCAVED.

DAMN, YOU'VE HEARD MY EXPRESSION.
NOW TELL ME WHAT KIND OF MAN I AM.

MANY OF US LIVE OUR LIVES
INCARCERATED, YET WE ARE TOLD WE

HAVE IT GOOD BECAUSE A FEW OF US HAVE MADE IT.

WE TRY SO HARD NOT TO COOPERATE WITH THE SYSTEMS DESIGN

BUT FROM LACK OF KNOWLEDGE, IT CONTROLS OUR MIND.

SO WHEN YOU THROW US INTO A GIGANTIC POT, IT MAY TAKE TIME TO AND TWO ALIKE NO ONE WANTS TO BE US BECAUSE OUR LIVES ARE BASED ON STEREOTYPES.

SEE, EVERYONE HAS THEIR OPINIONS, AND FOR MOST, I JUST LISTEN AND LAUGH BECAUSE EVERYONE TRIES TO PREDICT OUR FUTURE BUT DONT KNOW CRAP ABOUT OUR PAST.

DAMN, YOU'VE HEARD MY EXPRESSION. NOW TELL ME WHAT KIND OF MAN I AM.

IT IS INEVITABLE ONE DAY, WE WILL RISE BASED ON INNER STRENGTH

AND HEART ALONE, SEE, WE WEREN'T EVEN SUPPOSED TO SURVIVE, YET MANY WOULD LIKE TO BE OUR CLONE

BUT WE STILL KEEP GOING AND GOING STUCK SOMEWHERE NEAR THE

INTERSECTION KNOWING OUR DAY WILL COME ONCE WE CHANGE THE

WORLDS PERCEPTION.

HERE'S A CLUE I'M NOT A JEW.

DAMN, YOU'VE HEARD MY EXPRESSION.
NOW TELL ME WHAT KIND OF MAN I AM.

JASON MILLINE

February 22, 1983

God's view

The Still of the Night
a grasshopper's call
I look upon the quiet
earth
As GOD looks upon
ALL

Night

Night,
so still, so innocent
not even the sound of a voice heard
everyone sleeps
everyone dreams up a fantasy
cozy, the Night
very, very personal
wish it would forever stay
Night
if only it would
but then
there would be no morning...Hmmmmmmm

Black Pete/Sanchez/Poppie
11-9-1979
3:00 a.m.

NEXT CALLER PLEASE

HELLO,

HI, WHO'S THIS?

HI TOMMY, THIS IS SUMMER.

WHAT DO I LOOK UKE? WELL,

I'VE GOT BLUE EYES, LONG BLONDE HAIR,
AND I'M ABOUT 5'4 (LAUGH)

YOU LIKE THAT.

HI, MY NAME IS SUMMER

I'VE GOT LIGHT BROWN EYES, SANDY
BROWN HAIR, AND I'M 5'5"

HI, MY NAME IS SUMMER; WHO'S THIS?

I'M 5'6". I'VE GOT DARK BROWN EYES,
LONG BROWN CURLY HAIR

AND LONG LEGS.

HI, BILL; MY NAME IS SUMMER.

I'M 5'61/2 WITH RED HAIR AND DARK
GREEN EYES.

HI STEVE, MY NAME IS SUMMER.

I'M 57", 130 lbs. BROWN EYES, BLACK HAIR.

HI JOHN, WHAT DO YOU LOOK LIKE?

ME! I LOOK LIKE WHATEVER YOU WANT ME TO LOOK LIKE.

I LOOK LIKE YOUR DEEPEST, DARKEST, MOST INTIMATE FANTASY.

I'M BLACK; I'M WHITE, LATINO, ITALIAN, OR ASIAN.

I LOOK LIKE YOUR SISTER, IF YOU WANT ME TO,

I LOOK LIKE YOUR MOMMY WHEN YOU WERE SIX,

I LOOK LIKE YOUR WIFE, YOUR SECRETARY, YOUR MOTHER-IN-LAW,

AND THE GIRL NEXT DOOR,

(SMILE) YEAH, I LOOK LIKE HER TOO.

NEXT CALLER, PLEASE.

April 11, 1997
10:10 a.m.

"A Whole Lotta Thing"

What kind of thing is it?
Attitude; cornrows; Rhythm; Child please
It's a Black Thing.
Poppi Chulo, Siss, Siss, Mira Mommie,
it's a Puerto Rican Thing.
Way cool, pardon me, Pinkies up
it's a White Thing.
Cross Colors, Psychedelic hair, Irie Mon
it's a Jamaican Ting
Hey, Girl!
It's a Girl Thing.
Telephones
it's a Female Ting.
Opposites Attract
it's a Gender Thing.
Mi Amore, Bouquet, Jean Claude Michelle
It's a French Thing.
Hate whites, can't stand blacks
it's a Racist Thing.

Homeopathy, bella donna, Golden Seal
it's a Health Thing.
Breast Feeding
is a Natural Thing.
Left index Finger for the "F."
is a Typing Thing.
Camouflage, Atomic Bombs, Submarines
it's a War Thing.
Back door, top, bottom
it's a Gay Thing.

AIDS
is a For Real Thing.
life is a living
Cufie, Khimar, Salatt, Dawah
it's a Muslim Thing.
The Nile, Ganges, Himalayas, Confucius
it's a history Thing.
Monotheism, Polytheism I don't
eat pork, sacred is the cow
it's a Religious Thing.
Everybody's got their thing.
IT'S A WHOLE LOTTA THING!!

1997

Purpose

Like a stream of running water flowing from a mountain top traveling down, down, down, hitting up against rocks and flowing around them, overcoming pebbles along the way, leaving behind nutrients that will nourish and give life to the earth long after its departure, the stream has a purpose, to be bigger than a stream,

to reach the lake, a larger body of water, to become one with the ocean,

To join its flow with the rhythm of the sea's wave

to remain there for a time allotted by its creator until the time comes

for it to proceed unto its next journey.

Purpose….

What's yours,?

Look at where you've been and where you're going, and if you have any purpose at all, you will see that your purpose is no different from the stream of running water flowing from a mountain top traveling down, down, down.

Little Brothers

Come here, little brothers
Lend me your ears
I have a good news to tell you
Positive things to share.
I come with no weapons
you see, my hands are bare
I come with knowledge
and I give it to you, for you
all to share.

Come here, little brothers
my knowledge of truth, yeah
I'll share it with you.
Need I remind you that
You are strong.
Tell you that you were here
first, not by a freak of
nature or a curse
but, by the Almighty up above
who dare say that HE was
wrong.

August 1, 1997

Forgive Me, Father

Forgive me, Father for I have sinned
the worst part is I'd do it again
You have reason to be vexed
but my only sin is sex
As I lay on my back, knees, or atop him
The last thing I'm thinking is how to stop him
Forgive me, Father for I have sinned.

Sunday, June 18, 2023

God's an Indian

He that sat on the thrown was
an amber color, a Sardius, and Jasper Stone.
America the Great, God's Country as it is truly known.
We are copper,
Jasper, and copper are the same tone.

June 22, 2023

My Prayer Daily

All the borders are falling down, falling down, falling down

All the borders are falling down; my prayer daily.

Canadian border is falling down, falling down, falling down

Canadian border is falling down; my prayer daily.

Mexico border is falling down, falling down, falling down

Mexico border is falling down, my prayer daily.

All the criminals stay at bay, stay at bay, stay at bay

All the criminals stay at bay, my prayer daily.

June 21, 2023

Rise and Sing

Rising
Rah sing
Ra sing
Ra
Sing
Rise and sing
Sing unto Me, Israel.
Make a joyful noise.
Let it reach the heavens.
Psalms 98:4

June 22, 2023

This Land is Our Land

This land is our land; this land is our land, this land is our land

Woody was wrong when he wrote that song.

This land is our land, the Turtle Island; this land is our land.

"Through an act of congress, 'our' (their) government was giving away millions of acres of land in the West and the Midwest. Which meant that it was willing to undergird its white peasants from Europe with an economic floor."

Martin Luther King Jr.

June 21, 2023

To Be Chosen

The Chosen can never be unchosen
You think this is new
The Chosen can never be unchosen
The spirits, the Elohim, other nations, even the fallen knew
The chosen can never be unchosen
They tried to get us to turn our face from grace
wanting and wishing to be in our place
The chosen can never be unchosen
To get us off track, they told a lie
The moon could fall from its place in the sky
The Chosen are Chosen from birth until we die
The Most High proclaimed this true
The chosen can never be unchosen, no matter what we do.

"Who taught you to hate the texture of your hair?

Who taught you to hate the color of your skin to such an extent that you bleach it to look like the white man?

Who taught you to hate the shape of your nose and the shape of your lips?

Who taught you to hate yourself from the top of your head to the soles of your feet?

Who taught you to hate your own kind?

other.

Ask yourself, who taught you to hate being what G-d gave you?"

Malcolm X

June 21, 2023

Can't Change Me

You can't,
Tame me,
Rename me,
Rearrange me
Classify me,
Deny me,
Color me,
Negro me,
Black lives me,
African me,
It ain't me,
You can't change me;
Not Sorry.

Wombin

One rib to make me?
Then you should have one rib less.
Yet the same amount of rows sit in our chests
One rib to make me.
Let's put that theory to a test.
Scientific evidence will put it all to rest.
The wombin you see is more complex.
Wombin is not a man with a womb in fact,
A man is a woman with no womb intact.
Two nipples on you, but what do they do?
But, sit as reminders of your Maker too.
The genetic code for your scrotum,
Guess what, the ovaries wrote 'em.
The door to your vagina we sealed with a seam
Check your newborn boy to see what I mean.
The unholy cat, the patriarchy, got you believing a lie
They changed our image to an Albion in the sky.
Let's delve a little deeper, take a closer look.
At divine intervention that was told in The Book.
The story was told in days of old how the Hosts of heaven

with schematics in hand came up with a plan,

"Come let us go and make man."

Genesis 1:26

July 14, 1997

Ode to Frost

A man once stood before a dividing road
and wrote about the path he took
I have stood before the fork too
and had to decide what I would do.

June 28, 2023

Wachuma

Wachuma, Wachuma, Wachuma my deer.
Wachuma, Wachuma, I have no fear
the fire shows me Blue, red, orange antlers
Wachuma, Wachuma, Wachuma is here.

My Favorite Quotes

"Prepare for the valley when you're in the peak."

Keke LiBron

"The things you accept be the things you regret."

Ashanti

"A wise man can act a fool but a fool cannot act a wise man."

Muhammad Ali

But, I say, "A wise man can play a fool, but a fool cannot portray a wise man."

"Life is for the living."

Keke LiBron

"Most intellects do not believe in God but they fear us just the same."

Erykah Badu

"You can have whatever you want as long as it doesn't belong to another person."

Paul Tenaglia

Prosperity Teachings

"You're glistening."

Keke LiBron

"Whatever follows I AM becomes you."

I do not know who came up with this but I use it all of the time.

Early Writings

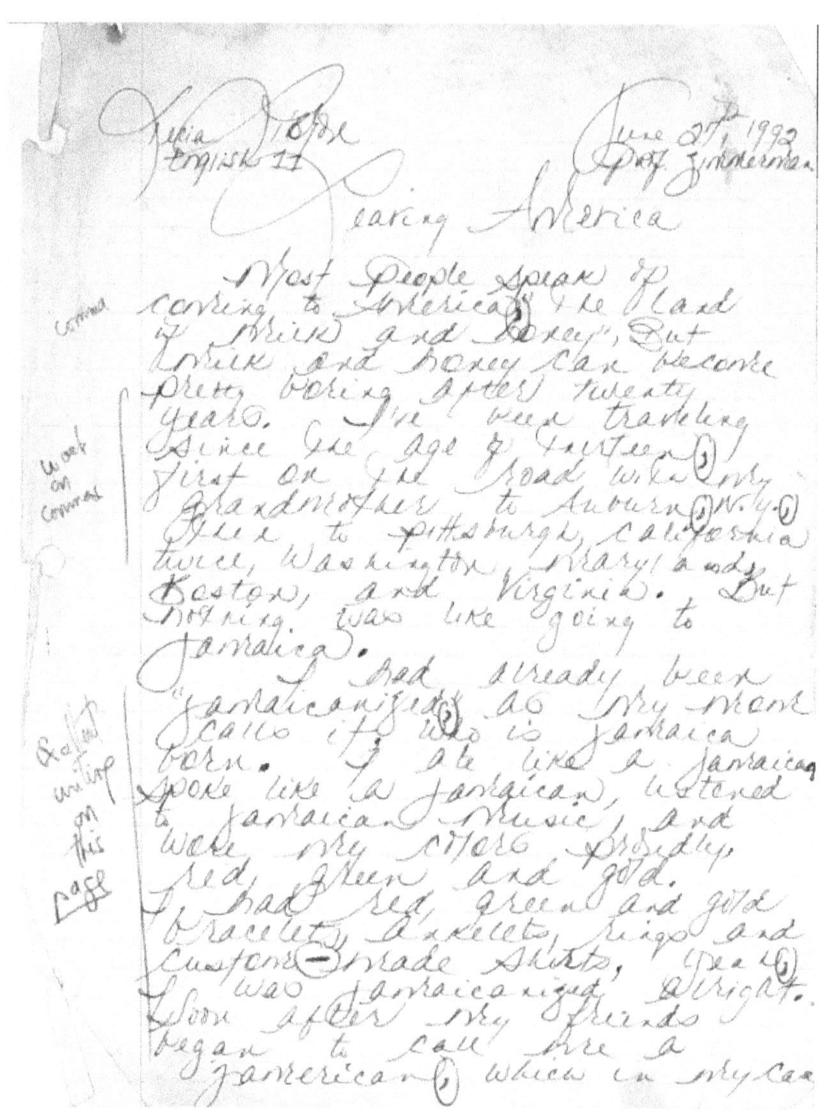

Kecia Moore
English II

June 27, 1992
Prof. Zimmerman

Leaving America

Most people speak of coming to America "the land of milk and honey", but milk and honey can become pretty boring after twenty years. I've been traveling since the age of fourteen, first on the road with my grandmother to Auburn, N.Y., then to Pittsburgh, California twice, Washington, Maryland, Boston, and Virginia. But nothing was like going to Jamaica.

I had already been "Jamaicanized" as my mom calls it, who is Jamaica born. I ate like a Jamaican, spoke like a Jamaican, listened to Jamaican music, and wore my colors proudly, red, green and gold. I had red, green and gold bracelets, anklets, rings and custom-made shirts. Yeah, I was Jamaicanized alright. Soon after my friends began to call me a Jamerican, which in my case

comma

work on commas

Excellent writing on this page

-2-

heart and American whose soul was truly Jamaican.

The next thing was to visit Jamaica, and in June 7, 1988 I did. It was everything I had imagined and everything I didn't.

The trees were taller than some of our biggest buildings and older too. The flowers came in colors I'd never seen before. They were so big and they were everywhere, purple, blue, green, red, and yellow; you name it, Jamaica had it.

My stepfather, who owns four houses in Jamaica, lives near a canefield so vast a person could easily become lost in it. The cane stood as tall as I (however tall I was then) and stretched out across miles. It seemed as though it had no begining and no end, or that the end touched the horizon every evening as I watched the sun set. Knowing no differently, I assumed this to

-3-

Lecia Rose

to be true. My mother stayed with me for a week. We went to a family reunion and then took in all the tourists attractions such as Bob Marleys (then new) statue and Devon house. We shopped for things to bring back home and I stocked up on shirts. I met some of her old friends, one who was the daughter of some rich guy in Jamaica. I had my toe nails done in tropical colors, of course, and dined at the best restaurants in Jamaica. I went out dancing only to find out they played more American songs than some of the clubs in America. My mother had to come back to the States because she had to work. A week later I would be leaving too. For the next week I ate mangos everyday, went to the market with my grandmother and hung out at my stepfather's restaurant.

Excellent paragraph structure — wonderful descriptions

fine writing

spell

no apostrophe

-4-

Kecia [illegible]

spell "ITS" with no apostrophe here

Jamaica was beautiful and the weather was great, but Jamaica had it's share of poverty also. Since the weather is nice all year round, I guess it's not so bad. The homeless built their own shelters out of wood. They had no heat, electricity or running water, but I guess it was home. To relieve themselves they went not far from their living quarters which left the area smelling like one of America's dirtiest sewers. Unlike tourists who only get to see the glamorized part of the places they visit I had the best of both worlds, the opportunity to see how the rich as well as the poor live.

fine

A / you're an excellent writer — and you are good at writing vivid descriptions

Very good

Della Pierce 10 December 16th 86
Speech Communication

Homework.

To Christmas

To Christmas is to love, to show love, it is a gathering of family and loved ones.

To Christmas:
all the holidays within the year you are the one which brings my family near. The loudest & laughter lingers in the air with Christmas carols being sung everywhere telling us that Christmas is near.... that Christmas is ~~near~~ here!

This Work Began In Rananchqua And It Concludes In Tenasi

The original place names of our land gives us details about the terrain, the trees, the water and what food or animals are abundant in a particular place.

Our words are vibrations that speak to our spirit. It is a language our DNA knows, remembers and will respond to. Let's use our words. It's time to vibrate Hiyah.

Peace in the highest.

Love, light and

Abundance,

Keke

www.ingramcontent.com/pod-product-compliance
Lightning Source LLC
LaVergne TN
LVHW011050110826
845149LV00015B/3430

* 9 7 8 1 9 6 2 2 2 4 1 2 3 *